How I Know My Dad is a Soldier

by

Dennis M. Johnson

AuthorHouse™
1663 Liberty Drive
Bloomington, IN 47403
www.authorhouse.com
Phone: 1 (800) 839-8640

Published by AuthorHouse 09/27/2017

ISBN: 978-1-4343-1181-8 (sc)

Print information available on the last page.

Any people depicted in stock imagery provided by Thinkstock are models,
and such images are being used for illustrative purposes only.
Certain stock imagery © Thinkstock.

This book is printed on acid-free paper.

authorHOUSE®

To all service members and their families

I can see my smile in the boots that he wears and shines.

He wears neat uniforms and hats.

He gets to drive cool trucks and jump out of airplanes.

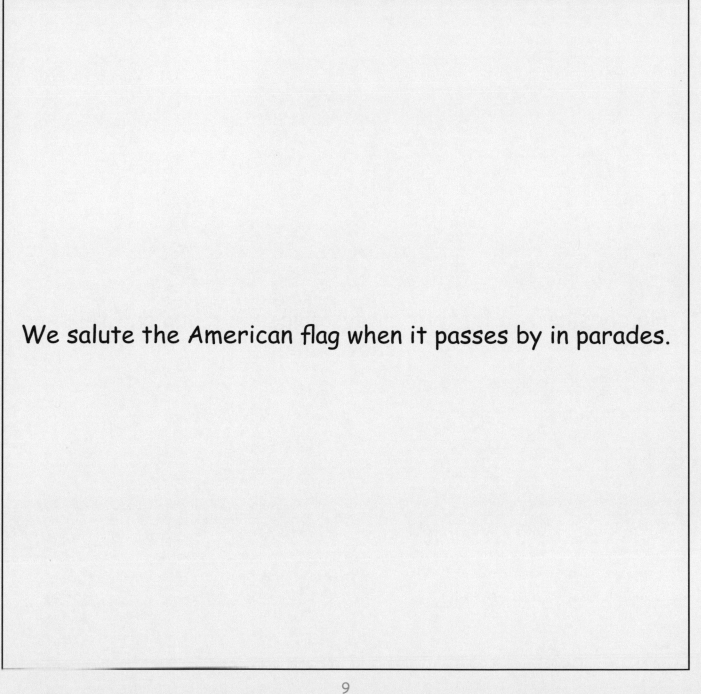

We salute the American flag when it passes by in parades.

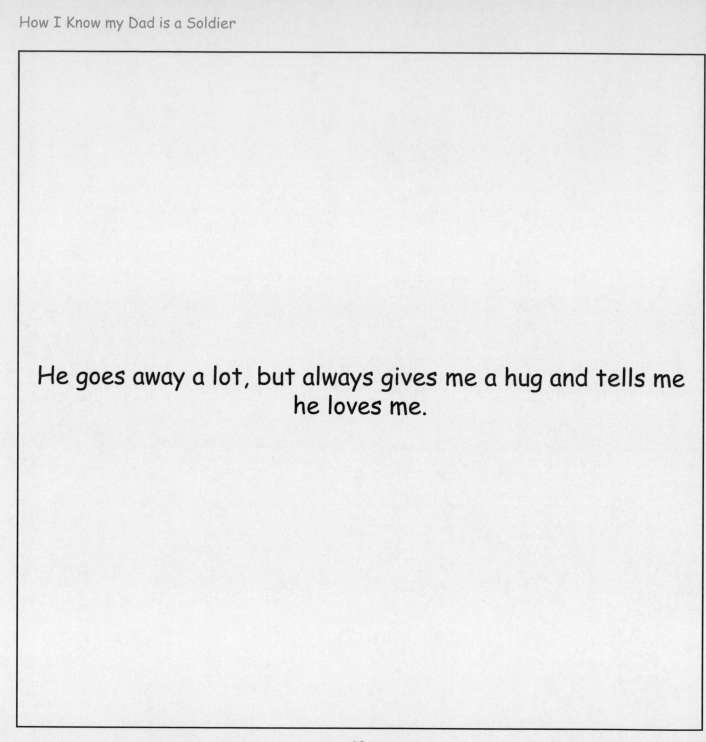

He goes away a lot, but always gives me a hug and tells me he loves me.

When he comes back he gives me another long hug and a kiss.

He gets a tear in his eye during the National Anthem.

But the number one reason I know my Dad is a Soldier, is....

Because my Mom is a Soldier too.

Printed in the United States
By Bookmasters